YOUR

HOPE

STORY

A Step-by-Step Guide to Help You
Write and Publish Your First Book

BRIAN DIXON

©2024 by Brian Dixon

Published by hope*books
2217 Matthews Township Pkwy
Suite D302
Matthews, NC 28105
www.hopebooks.com

hope*books is a division of hope*media

Printed in the United States of America

First paperback edition.
Paperback ISBN: 979-8-89185-104-7
Hardcover ISBN: 979-8-89185-105-4
Ebook ISBN: 979-8-89185-106-1

Library of Congress Number: 2024944620

hope*books
hopebooks.com
Because the world needs your hope filled
words now more than ever.

TABLE OF CONTENTS

INTRODUCTION

Someday I'll Write a Book

Have you ever thought to yourself, "Someday I'll write a book?"

You know that you have something to say and a story to share. You look around and see injustice, pain, and a longing for hope. You know you can help. You have something that could encourage others, a story that could make others feel less alone.

The only problem is that sharing your story can take a lot of work. It takes time, effort, and a clear path. That's probably why you haven't done it yet. But the idea just won't go away.

That's why you picked up this book. You know that you have a calling on your life. And part of that calling is sharing your story. It's really exciting if you think about it. But, the truth is it can be really scary too.

After working with thousands of members in hope*writers, our online community for writing, and helping hundreds of authors write and publish their books with hope*-

books, I know from experience that right now you have two options when it comes to writing and publishing your book.

Your Two Options

There are two options when it comes to writing and publishing your book: you can wait or you can get to work. That's it. As creatives, we tend to live in our heads, overanalyze, and needlessly complicate decisions. But the truth is usually pretty simple. You can wait or you can work.

Waiting feels comfortable. It's a story you might be telling yourself right now, "I'll wait a little longer for the right time. I'll save up some time, money, and my best stories for the future." Doesn't that sound wonderful? You're off the hook and you don't have to write your book right now—it's a problem for "future you." The challenge with waiting is that it doesn't get you any closer to your goal. You can't save up time. Time just keeps moving forward. If you want to predict your future, just look at yesterday. Did you have more time yesterday? Did you have more money yesterday? What if all this delay is actually putting off something really important? What if the waiting isn't building towards something but missing out on something?

Waiting, even though it feels comfortable, is often the opposite of progress. It's a distraction from what you want to be true. It's easier to choose that path than to choose the hard path, actually sitting down and getting it down—starting to write your story today. Why the urgency? Because there are people right now who need to hear your story. There are people in pain who need you to get to work. Now.

Which brings us to our second option. Getting started today. Actually getting to work right now. Start telling your story. Start putting in the time today, instead of trying to save up time for someday. Think about the progress you could make if you put in a little bit of time writing part of your story every day for the rest of the month. How much closer would you be to having written your book? Or if you are "really busy," what if you just decided to take one hour a week on Saturday afternoons for the next year or so to work on your book? What if you woke up a few minutes earlier tomorrow morning? What if, as many of our hope*-books authors have done, you find the "cracks of time" in your life like in the carpool line, at the soccer game, while waiting for an appointment to write your story down? Do you think you'd be further along than you are right now?

Everything could change for you when you get to work.

Here's the truth: once your story is written down, someone else (like a developmental editor) can clean it up.

But no one can write your story for you. If it is going to be, it's time to take 100% responsibility. If you've been dreaming about writing and publishing your hope*story, getting to work now is the key to making this dream a reality. And this book you are reading right now can help you get started today. This is the SIGN you've been waiting for, my friend. This is your wake-up call. The time is now.

Will you decide right now to work instead of wait? The choice is yours.

You Don't Have to Be an Expert

Now that you've decided to move forward and begin writing your book, it's totally normal for an overwhelming wave of unhelpful thoughts and fears to come flooding in. Imposter syndrome. The comparison monster. A general feeling of overwhelm. A voice inside saying, "Who do you think you are? You don't have what it takes! No one will want to read YOUR story. Shame. Doubt. Fear. Boo!!!"

Sound too dramatic? Maybe not.

I know what it's like to face that fear and write my story anyway. I've helped thousands of writers share their stories. And I'm here to help you too.

If you're feeling unqualified to write a book and share your story, remember that you don't need to be an expert. You don't have to be a guru; all you need to be is authentically yourself. Your unique journey of tragedy and triumph, struggle and success, is more than enough. You hold the truth of your own life—no one else is more qualified to tell your story. Forget about fancy degrees or special certifications. You don't need a massive social media following or a huge email list. Your personal story is your testimony, the powerful truth of what you've seen, experienced, overcome, and lived through.

"I was lost, but now I'm found. I was blind, but now I see. I was broken, but now I'm healed."

This is the power of your story. It's unique to you. And no one else has the same story that you do.

We live in an age of "guru fatigue." Every podcast and news program has some expert telling us the three steps to this or the five keys to that. But so many of these prepackaged cookie-cutter answers feel inauthentic. In a world of 30-second experts, people look for deep truths.

The kind of truth that only a friend will tell you.

A guru will tell you what to do, but a friend will share what she did. An expert can overwhelm you with statistics, but a friend can share her heart. And that's what readers are looking for. The truth. We don't need another guru on a hill telling us how to live, we need a kind companion along-side us to show the way that worked for them. That's why it is so powerful and important for you to share your story. Your "testimony" can be the key that unlocks the prison for someone else.

Your Story Matters

By sharing your story—telling us where you've been, what you've experienced, how it felt, what you tried, what worked, and what didn't—you connect with a reader who can relate to your experience.

In a world of fake, the truth shines bright.

Your reader needs to know the truth.

If she's struggling in her marriage and thinking about giving up, she needs to hear your story: how you were exactly where she is, what you did to move forward, and how you made it work.

If she's overwhelmed in her life, just trying to make it through another day, she doesn't need another productivity expert. She needs to hear how you decided to look in the mirror and live. Your story of struggle can be what helps set her free.

If she's struggling to communicate with her teenager, she's not looking for some weathered parenting guru. She's looking for what to do now, and you can share how you broke through and made a connection with your own teenager. She just wants to know that she is not alone. She is holding out for hope: the hope that you have to share by telling your story!

You can tell her it's going to be okay because you are okay. You made it through, and now she can too. What a gift it could be to share your hope*story with her!

The Three Writing Traps

Once you begin to see what's possible when you share your hope*story, it's really tempting to just get started. Time to get to work, right? Don't worry, we'll get there, but first, let's talk about the process of actually writing a book. Because this is where a lot of enthusiasm can lead to overwhelm and discouragement.

Having helped first-time authors write and publish their books for over ten years now, I've seen firsthand the many pitfalls authors can fall into and the many pit stops that can get you stuck. Let's identify these traps and talk through how to avoid them, so you can write your book without getting stuck.

The first trap is the unfocused manuscript. Most first-time authors believe that the way to write a book is to sit down and start writing. But great books aren't written; they are built.

Writing a book doesn't just happen randomly. It's kind of like building a house. You don't just start swinging a hammer and suddenly have a beautiful home. You start with a blueprint. Then you create a budget. You collect the materials, put them in order, and bring in others to help in the process. This systematic approach results in a well-built beautiful home. And the same is true with your book. Simply sitting down to write and pushing through doesn't work. Instead, you need to follow the five proven steps that our authors at hope*books follow every day to write and publish their book in record time. And you, my friend, can do the same. (I'll teach you the whole "book building" system in the second section of this book.)

Distraction, otherwise known as "shiny object syndrome," is the second trap I see first-time authors fall into.

Changing your mind. A lot. Starting one project, then trying another. Or even worse, trying to write several books at the same time. Writing one non-fiction book AND one fiction book AND one children's book AND one guided journal all at the same time. Going from no books to five books at the same time is a recipe for never finishing one book. So how do you avoid this shiny object syndrome? The solution is FOCUS. Follow one course until success. Trust the process and complete this one book first. The lessons you'll learn, the process you'll follow, and the skills you'll develop will help you with book number two! Don't worry about that now, just focus on this first book .

And finally, the third trap I see many first-time authors fall into is isolation. Trying to white knuckle your way to a finished book completely on your own. Writing alone is a recipe for overwhelm, frustration, and quitting. Instead, you need community. A group of other authors who know what it is like. A clear path to follow and a supportive community where you can ask your "ungoogleable" questions. A place like hopewriters.com. Finding your writing friends will help you actually finish your book because you'll have the support, understanding, and encouragement you need. When you have others who are walking this journey with you, it's less hard and a lot more fun.

So are you ready to get started? Here's what you'll discover in this book. First, we'll talk through the reasons you need to write your story. We'll clarify your "why." Second, we'll walk through the how, the five-step book-building process to help you write your book in record time. And finally, we'll examine the three ways to get your book published—so you can share your hope*story!

SECTION 1

WHY WRITE YOUR STORY

Before we walk through the five steps of writing your book, let's get very clear on your "why." Why write your book? When you are clear on your why, you'll be able to push past the inevitable setbacks, roadblocks, and detours. There are three reasons to write your story. As you read through this section, decide which will be YOUR reason for writing your hope*story!

Writing Your Story Helps You Live a Better Story

The first reason to write your story is for yourself. Your own personal fulfillment. In fact, writing your story helps you live a better story. Reflecting on your past helps you create a better future. This alone is worth it. Imagine going through the entire process of writing and publishing your book and then no one else ever reads it. It doesn't hit the

New York Times Bestseller list. It doesn't lead to fame and fortune. You don't make millions of dollars. Instead, all you get is the personal satisfaction of having written your story. Would it be worth it? I want to argue that it would be. In fact, processing your past—putting pen to paper—can be transformative. Taking the time to reflect on your experiences can lead to a transformed life.

It's similar to the power of journaling, where you reflect on daily experiences. But writing your hope*story takes it to another level—it helps you solidify your life's philosophy. That's right. We're going deep, my friend. By actually writing and publishing your book, you're documenting your "life's philosophy." The writing process is a perspective clarifier, crystalizing what you believe and the reasons behind your actions both in the past and in the future.

Sometimes we act or react in certain ways without knowing why. Writing your story allows you to examine the "why." This can be a transformative process. As you begin to tell your story and share your life's philosophy through the written word, you'll uncover lessons you've learned, challenges you've overcome, and trials you've survived.

Yes, this can be a scary process, and sometimes it means getting additional help from a pastor or counselor. But I want to encourage you that it is worth it. It's like spring cleaning for the soul. By taking the time to process and write your story, you transform into a new person, and that alone is worth the time and pain of writing your book!

Writing Your Story Helps Other People

A second reason to write your hope*story is for other people. What you've been through isn't wasted when it's shared with somebody else. The challenges you've faced and overcome might be in your past, but they're in somebody else's present. Right now, countless people are facing a challenge similar to the one you overcame years ago. You had to grind your way through to figure it out. You didn't have a roadmap. But now that you've made it through, you can look back, reach out your hand, and help others. Your book can be the roadmap for someone else to follow to freedom.

The pain you've been through, the personal challenges you've faced, and the heartache you've endured are not wasted. Other people need to hear your story. You now know what to avoid, what to expect, the action to take, and the belief to embrace. This knowledge is a gift, not to be hoarded but to be shared with others. Your story could be the key that unlocks the prison someone else is trapped in.

It might be hard to picture it now, especially if you're not used to sharing on social media, but I want you to know that there are people who are searching every single day for helpful content to transform their lives. Content that you have stored up in your head and your heart.

Let's take parenting as an example. You've successfully launched two kids out into the world, but you remember what it was like to walk through those teenage years. In fact, there were many challenges that you faced and overcame. But that's in your past. Other people, however, are looking for those lessons you've learned today. You had to struggle your way through, but now you have tips and strategies that can help other people. If you were to share those strategies, tell your story, and share your advice, some lives could be transformed through your experience. They wouldn't make the same mistakes you made because they now have the roadmap you created for them.

Or let's take the area of faith. Maybe you've been through a faith crisis and you really struggled to figure out what you believe, but through your own personal story and reflection, you've come to a level of confidence and assuredness about what you believe and why you choose to live the way you live. And yet others are questioning their faith right now, skeptical and doubt-filled. What if they were to hear your story and it led to a transformation in their life?

How meaningful would it be to know someone was encouraged by reading your story? That your small story made a big impact on their life? That is the power of helping others by writing your story.

Writing Your Story Leaves a Legacy

A third reason to write and publish your story is to leave a legacy. One day, you won't be here anymore. Someday, far into the future, your grandchildren and your great-grand-children will have questions. They'll want to know where they came from. They'll want to know about the past. They'll want to know about their great-grandmother. What if you could send them a love letter? What if you could help them avoid some of the pain that you've had to walk through? What if you could share your life lessons far into the future to make an impact on those who you'll never meet? This is what's possible when you write your story. This is the power of writing and publishing your story.

Recently, we were going through some old boxes, and we discovered a self-published book from the 1960s by George T. Stevens. George was my wife's great-grandfather. In 1961, he and his wife worked together to write a short book called *True Revival*. It recounted what it was like to be a traveling evangelist in the 1960s. In this book, he shared his life philosophy, stories of struggle and overcoming, stories of crisis and personal growth, stories of doubt, and of finding faith.

The funny thing is George had no idea that one day, more than sixty years in the future, his great-granddaughter would be reading his book. Isn't that amazing?

The same can be true for you! By writing and publishing your story now, you'll be leaving a special gift for your family in the future. You're creating a timeless legacy they can read for generations to come. By writing your story, you're not only preserving your memories and wisdom but providing a precious gift for future generations. Your story becomes a bridge from the present to the future and from the future to the past. Your book can offer them guidance, wisdom, and insight long after you're gone.

Bonus: Writing Your Story Creates a Side Income

Perhaps a surprising reason to write your story is that you can create a side income by selling your books and building a career around your story. We call this career being a "hope*writer." And yes, the pay can be really amazing. I know this might sound a little far-fetched right now, but did you know that writing and publishing your story can actually pay really well? I've worked with dozens of clients who have built six-figure businesses—and they all started by sharing their stories. Here's how the path from side income, to sustainable income, to six-figure income usually works.

First, you have a desire to write your book. As you begin the journey, you start sharing your stories—usually by posting them on Facebook or Instagram or writing them on a personal blog. Practicing your writing by publishing your words helps you better craft exactly what you want to say.

As you begin to share your words, mostly for yourself but also to encourage others, you start to develop an audience. At first, these might be friends on Facebook, but over time, you develop a fan base.

Through comments and replies you begin to hear from others whose lives are being transformed by the lessons you're sharing. The more you share, the more your audience continues to grow. You launch a website with yourname.com and begin building your email list by giving away a free resource to your new subscribers.

Your audience continues to grow as you create helpful content. There's a back-and-forth with your audience: they ask a question, and you answer by creating content. Eventually, it makes sense to take this content and repackage it into paid products. These include your book, an online course, or even a paid membership community. These products begin to generate revenue—first side income, then sustainable income, and then eventually six figures of income.

In fact, the average six-figure, full-time author has eight streams of revenue. These income streams might include book sales, merchandise, online courses, materials and workbooks, group coaching, sponsorships, one-on-one coaching, affiliates, paid memberships, consulting, mastermind groups, licensing, speaking engagements, viewership, and certification programs. Once you've published your book and are generating different income streams, we call this being an "authorpreneur." I know this might sound like something in the distant future, but it is possible, once you begin sharing your story.

P.S. If you're curious about the 15 income streams you can develop by sharing your story, scan the QR code here or visit hopebooks.com/income.

So there you have it. Four reasons to write your story and publish your book. These reasons include your own personal fulfillment, the value of helping others, leaving a legacy for future generations, and yes, even building side income as an author.

So what about you? Which "why" is right for you? What is your reason for writing your story?

SECTION 1 WORKSHEET

Writing Your Story Helps You Live a Better Story

1. **Personal Fulfillment:**

   What personal satisfaction do you hope to gain from writing your story?

   _____

   _____

   _____

   _____

   What life lessons or philosophies do you want to solidify through the process of writing your story?

   _____

   _____

   _____

   _____

   How might writing your story transform your way of thinking, acting, and living?

   _____

   _____

   _____

   _____

2. **Self-Discovery:**

   Are there aspects of your past you've never fully explored or understood?

   _____

   _____

   _____

   _____

   What are some key moments in your life that have shaped who you are today?

   _____

   _____

   _____

   _____

   How do you hope to grow or change as a person through the process of writing your story?

   _____

   _____

   _____

   _____

Writing Your Story Helps Other People

1. **Impact on Others:**

   What challenges have you faced that others might be struggling with right now?

   _____

   _____

   _____

What lessons or strategies have you learned that could help others if shared?

_____

_____

_____

_____

How would it feel to know that your story has made a positive impact on someone else's life?

_____

_____

_____

_____

2. **Contribution:**

Who do you think would gain the most from hearing your story?

_____

_____

_____

_____

In what ways can your story provide guidance, hope, or encouragement to others?

_____

_____

_____

_____

How do you envision your story being used as a tool for others' growth and transformation?

_____

_____

_____

_____

Writing Your Story Leaves a Legacy

1. **Legacy:**

   What do you want future generations to know about you and your life?

   _____

   _____

   _____

   _____

   What do you hope your great-grandchildren will learn from your story?

   _____

   _____

   _____

   _____

Bonus: Writing Your Story Creates a Side Income

1. **Financial Potential:**

   How does the idea of generating a side income from your story appeal to you?

   _____

   _____

   _____

   _____

   What types of income streams (e.g., book sales, online courses, speaking engagements) interest you the most?

   _____

   _____

   _____

   _____

   What is your long-term vision for your story and its potential to create a sustainable income?

   _____

   _____

   _____

   _____

Reflecting on these questions will help you gain clarity on your motivations for writing your story, guiding you toward a purpose that will sustain you throughout the writing process.

SECTION 2

HOW TO WRITE YOUR STORY

Now it's time to write your story. You've decided to stop waiting and get to work. You're clear on your "why." Now let's talk through the "how." I've compiled the five essential steps in the process based on my experience helping hundreds of authors write and publish their books. As mentioned before, a book is not written, it is built. Having a clear blueprint for your book allows you to fill in the gaps as you go instead of getting stuck and guessing what to do next. It makes it clear exactly what is missing and what needs to be written. A blueprint helps you overcome potential overwhelm because you know what to write now and what to write next. We begin with the XYZ Statement, then the Transformation Tale, then the detailed chapter outline, then the model chapter, and finally, the full manuscript. Following these five steps will give you the clarity you need to actually finish writing your book.

Step 1: Your XYZ Statement

The first step in writing your book is to craft your "XYZ Statement." This is a simple, three-part framework that clarifies these important elements:

1. The person your book is for. (X)
2. The problem your book addresses. (Y)
3. The promise your book offers. (Z)

Now I know what you might be thinking, "I thought I was just trying to write my story. Why do I have to have a clear vision for the kind of book I want to write?" That's a really great question. Before we walk through the process of crafting your own XYZ statement, let's talk about why it's so important to narrow this down. There are three reasons:

First, your XYZ Statement helps you write your book. It helps you decide what to include and what to leave out. You are writing your book for a real person with a real problem. This XYZ Statement serves as a focus filter, helping you have clarity as you write your book for your ideal reader. Crafting an XYZ statement helps clarify your narrative's purpose, audience, and promise. By defining your XYZ statement, you set a clear direction for your writing, ensuring your story resonates with the right people and delivers a meaningful message. This clarity will guide you throughout the writing process, making your message more impactful and effective.

Second, an XYZ Statement helps you describe your book. It makes it easy to explain what your book is about. Perhaps you are familiar with the "elevator pitch." It's a 5-second description of what you do, that you're able to say in just enough time before reaching your floor in an elevator. When you write and publish your book, inevitably someone will ask, "What is your book about?" Your XYZ Statement is the answer. Here's an example, "You know how X (person) struggles with Y (problem)? My book helps X (person) overcome Y (problem) so they can Z (promise)." Memorizing your XYZ Statement to help you explain what your book is about will be invaluable when others ask about your book, when you talk about your book on social media, and when you share about your book on podcast interviews.

Third, a clear XYZ Statement helps you sell more books. When people know who your book is for, the problem it addresses, and the solution it provides, they will lean in. They will want to buy your book. They'll want to tell that one friend about the book because it is perfectly suited for her! A clear XYZ Statement helps make your book "googleable" and referrable. If the person, problem, and promise of the book are clear, then a quick search on Google will lead someone to your book. Also, when someone has that specific problem in their life, others will be able to recommend your book, referring you and your work to that specific person who has that specific problem.

Even though you may want your book to help everyone, clearly identifying your one ideal reader will help write your book, describe your book, and sell your book. So now that you are clear on why you need an XYZ Statement for your book, it's time to craft your XYZ Statement. We'll start with your people, the X that your book is for. Then we'll clearly identify the Y, the problem that your book addresses in the 11 key domains of life. Finally, we'll define the Z, the promise that your book offers.

X: *Clarifying the Person Your Story Is For*

The first element of the XYZ statement is identifying your target audience—the "X." This step is about understanding who you are writing for. A common mistake I see first-time authors make is writing a book for themselves instead of writing for a reader. Yes, in many ways your book is about you—after all, it is your hope*story. But, you want other people to read it, right? And you want those readers to be impacted? So before you begin, it's important to consider exactly who these readers are. The more specifically you define your ideal reader, the more intentional you can be in crafting a book that best helps her.

The best way I've found to narrow down exactly who your reader is involves clearly identifying the demographics and psychographics of your ideal reader. Demographics refer to the observable characteristics of your reader, such as gender, age, location, and occupation. Psychographics are the less observable traits, including values, dreams, desires, hopes, and fears. When you are clear on both the demographics and psychographics of your ideal reader, you'll know exactly what to include and what to leave out of your book because it is tailored for them.

Deciding on your reader's characteristics can be tricky, especially if you want to write a book that helps "everyone." While this might be true, it's important to focus on one ideal reader when writing your book. This clarity will guide your decisions about which stories to include and which to leave out. If you're having trouble deciding, just think of a real-life friend you'd want to read your book!

Demographics

First, we'll start with your readers' demographics. Generally, these are the externally observable characteristics of your reader.

- **Marital Status**: Is your ideal reader single, dating, engaged, married, divorced, or widowed?

- **Gender**: Tailor your messaging to resonate with the specific experiences, challenges, and perspectives of a man or woman.

- **Age**: The life stage, challenges, and priorities of your audience.

- **Location**: Geographic details can influence reader behavior, needs, and access to resources or services. Cultural nuances based on location can also affect how your message is received.

- **Income**: Income levels can affect purchasing power, lifestyle choices, and the types of problems your audience might face or solutions they seek.

- **Occupation**: Provides context about their daily routines, professional challenges, and aspirations, which can influence their interests and needs.

Many of our clients struggle to narrow down these demographics, usually because they want to write a book that helps everybody. So I understand if this process can feel difficult. But let's push through this together.

DEMOGRAPHICS WORKSHEET

To help you narrow down the demographics of your ideal reader, please select one option from each category below. If none of the options fit, feel free to choose your own.

1. **Marital Status**
   - Single
   - Married
   - Divorced
   - Choose your own: _____

2. **Gender**
   - Male
   - Female

3. **Age**
   - 20s
   - 30s
   - 40s
   - 50s
   - 60s+

4. **Location**
   - Urban
   - Suburban
   - Rural

5. Income

- Below $30,000

- $30,000 - $60,000

- $60,000 - $100,000

- Above $100,000

- Choose your own: _____

6. Occupation

- Teacher

- Small Business Owner

- Corporate Professional

- Healthcare Worker

- Choose your own: _____

EXAMPLE DEMOGRAPHIC PROFILES

Here are a few examples to help you visualize your ideal reader:

Example 1:

My book is for a single woman in her late thirties who lives in Kansas City. She makes $55,000 a year as a middle school math teacher.

Example 2:

My book is for a married man in his early fifties who lives in San Diego. He makes $270,000 a year as the owner of a chain of Mexican restaurants.

Example 3:

My book is for a divorced woman in her mid-forties who lives in a suburban area. She makes $75,000 a year as a nurse.

By selecting the most fitting options for each category, you can create a detailed profile of your ideal reader. This will help you tailor your book to meet their specific needs and interests, making your message more impactful and relatable.

Psychographics

Now, let's dive into the psychographics of your ideal reader. Psychographics refers to the unobservable, more nuanced aspects of your reader's life. These include values, interests, hobbies, concerns, hopes, fears, dreams, and desires. While demographics give us a snapshot of who your reader is on the outside, psychographics reveal who they are on the inside—their motivations, behaviors, and attitudes.

Understanding the psychographics of your audience is crucial because it allows you to connect with them on a deeper, more personal level. It helps you tailor your message to resonate with their core beliefs and aspirations, address their deepest concerns, and inspire their greatest dreams. When you know what makes your reader tick, you can create content that truly speaks to their heart.

Have fun imagining who your ideal reader is! Picture their day-to-day life, what excites them, what keeps them up at night, and what they dream about. This exercise will not only help you better understand your audience but also make your writing process more engaging and meaningful. Let's explore the inner world of your readers and discover what truly drives them.

- **Values**: These are the core principles that guide your audience's decisions, behaviors, and lifestyle. By aligning your message with these values, you can deeply resonate with their sense of identity.

- **Interests**: What your audience enjoys doing in their free time can give you ideas for what to reference, what stories to tell, and what details they'll care about.

- **Hobbies**: What activities do they do for fun? Understanding hobbies can help in creating relatable content or services.

- **Concerns**: Identifying what worries your audience allows you to address these fears directly and offer solutions.

- **Hopes**: Knowing what your audience aspires to achieve or become can guide the promise of your message.

- **Fears**: Understanding fears helps in empathizing with your audience and crafting messages that reassure and motivate.

- **Dreams**: These represent the ideal life or achievements your audience envisions for themselves. Messaging that connects with these dreams can be highly motivating.

- **Desires**: Consider the tangible wants that drive your audience's daily decisions and preferences. By tapping into these desires, you can make your message more compelling.

When you clarify the psychographics of your ideal reader, you paint a fuller picture of exactly who you are writing for and how she'll respond to your words.

PSYCHOGRAPHICS WORKSHEET

To help you more clearly identify your ideal reader, choose the psychographic descriptor options on this worksheet that most resonate with the person you are writing for.

1. **Values**
   - Faith
   - Family
   - Integrity
   - Community
   - Choose your own: _____

2. **Interests**
   - Reading
   - Volunteering
   - Traveling
   - Outdoor Activities
   - Choose your own: _____

3. **Hobbies**
   - Gardening
   - Cooking
   - Hiking
   - Crafting
   - Choose your own: _____

4. **Concerns**
   - Financial Stability
   - Health and Wellness

- Family Relationships
- Personal Growth
- Choose your own: _____

5. **Hopes**
   - Building a Strong Family
   - Growing in Faith
   - Achieving Career Success
   - Contributing to Community
   - Choose your own: _____

6. **Fears**
   - Failure
   - Rejection
   - Financial Insecurity
   - Illness
   - Choose your own: _____

7. **Dreams**
   - Leading a Purposeful Life
   - Traveling the World
   - Making a Significant Impact
   - Building a Lasting Legacy
   - Choose your own: _____

8. **Desires**
   - Immediate Financial Relief
   - Work-Life Balance
   - Family Harmony
   - Discovering Her Calling
   - Choose your own: _____

EXAMPLE PSYCHOGRAPHIC PROFILES

Example 1:

My reader values family and integrity. She is interested in reading and volunteering. She enjoys gardening as a hobby. She is concerned about financial stability and family relationships. Her hopes are to build a strong family and grow in faith. She fears financial insecurity. Her dreams include leading a purposeful life and building a lasting legacy. She desires immediate financial relief and stronger personal relationships.

Example 2:

My reader values faith and community. He is interested in outdoor activities and traveling. He enjoys hiking and cooking as hobbies. He is concerned about health and wellness. His hopes are to achieve career success and contribute to the community. He fears failure and rejection. His dreams include making a significant impact and traveling the world. He desires work-life balance and personal recognition.

Example 3:

My reader values integrity and faith. She is interested in reading and outdoor activities. She enjoys crafting and hiking as hobbies. She is concerned about her health and medical debt. Her hopes are to grow in faith and live a healthy life. She fears illness and financial insecurity. Her dreams include leading a purposeful life and building a lasting legacy. She desires stronger personal relationships and a long, peace-filled life.

Now it's your turn. Put together your ideal reader psychographic profile based on the worksheet and examples above:

_____

_____

_____

_____

_____

_____

Bring it all together

Now that you have the specific demographics and psychographics of the person you envision reading your book, let's bring it all together and create your ideal reader profile. This clarity will help you tailor your content to effectively meet their needs and interests.

Here are a few examples to help write your own "Ideal Reader Profile":

Example 1:

My reader is a single woman in her late thirties who lives in Kansas City. She makes $55,000 a year as a middle school math teacher. She values family and integrity, is interested in reading and volunteering, and enjoys gardening as a hobby. She is concerned about financial stability and family relationships. Her hopes are to build a strong family and grow in faith. She fears financial insecurity and illness. Her dreams include leading a purposeful life and building a lasting legacy. She desires immediate financial relief and stronger personal relationships.

Example 2:

My reader is a married man in his early fifties who lives in San Diego. He makes $270,000 a year as the owner of a chain of Mexican restaurants. He values faith and community, is interested in outdoor activities and traveling, and enjoys hiking and cooking as hobbies. He is concerned about health, wellness, and personal growth. His hopes are to achieve career success and contribute to the community. He fears failure and rejection. His dreams include making a significant impact and traveling the world. He desires work-life balance and personal recognition.

Example 3:

My reader is a divorced woman in her mid-forties who lives in a suburban area. She makes $75,000 a year as a nurse. She values integrity and faith, is interested in reading and outdoor activities, and enjoys crafting and hiking as hobbies. She is concerned about health, wellness, and financial stability. Her hopes are to grow in faith and achieve career success. She fears illness and financial insecurity. Her dreams include leading a purposeful life and building a lasting legacy. She desires stronger personal relationships and immediate financial relief.

Now it's your turn (Mad Libs style):

My reader is a _____ _____ in
                 [insert marital status]   [man/woman]

_____ _____ who lives in _____.
[his/her]   [insert age range]   [insert location]

_____ makes _____ a year as a
[He/She]   [insert income]

_____. _____
       [insert profession]   [He/She]

values _____, is interested in _____,
        [insert values]   [insert interests]

and enjoys _____. _____ is concerned about
        [insert hobbies]   [He/She]

_____. _____ hopes are to _____.
[insert concerns]   [His/Her]   [insert hopes]

_____ fears _____. _____
[He/She]   [insert fears]   [His/Her]

dreams include _____. _____ desires
          [insert dreams]   [He/She]

_____.
[insert immediate desires]

Now rewrite your description into one complete paragraph:

_____

_____

_____

_____

_____

_____

_____

_____

_____

_____

Use this template to craft a detailed and personalized profile of your ideal reader, ensuring you have a clear understanding of who you are writing for. This will help you create content that resonates deeply with your audience.

You, Three Years Ago

If you are having trouble deciding who to write your book for, I have a quick hack that has helped countless members of our online writing community, hopewriters.com. It's simply this: Write for yourself three years ago. You already know the struggles you were facing and the challenges you overcame over the last few years. Three years ago is not that far away, but if you really think about it, you've been through so much. So look back on your calendar. Review your old journals. Look at your social media posts and consider what you were going through three years ago. Now imagine that you could write the perfect bookYOU needed three years ago. Wouldn't that have been amazing? That's exactly the opportunity that you have now. So go back and articulate your own demographics and psychographics from three years ago. Then use this reader profile for your XYZ Statement.

Y: *Identifying the Problem Your Book Addresses*

Now that you are clear on the reader for your book, it's time to decide on the specific problem your book will address.

One of the biggest challenges my clients face is narrowing down their unique message. I understand why this is difficult because I struggle with it too. There's so much I want to talk about. I want to share my faith, discuss how I set goals for my future, offer tips and strategies on scheduling and focus, and, of course, talk about my family. All this is in addition to my field of writing and publishing books. So, what do we do? How do you narrow down and figure out that one core message you have to share? The truth is, there are all sorts of topics you could intelligently write about. Family. Friendships. Faith and more. But a great book focuses on just one topic.

That's why it is so important to FOCUS on one topic for the book you are writing. Choose one life lesson you've learned so you can help countless others.

So how do you decide what that one message will be?

To help you clarify your Y, I want to introduce you to the 11 domains of life. I've created these helpful categories to help define the specific problem that your book addresses. Eleven domains of life where people are seeking guidance to help them live a more meaningful life.

To further focus the topic of your book, I've divided each of these 11 life domains into three subdomains, giving you a total of 33 options to choose from. These are the main categories that book buyers seek for guidance and help in their lives. While there are many other topics not included in these 33, if you desire to share your story of hope, I highly recommend choosing one of these options.

Each of these 11 domains is divided even further into 3 subdomains, giving you a total of 33 options to choose from when deciding on the topic for your book. These domains are:

Domain	Subdomain 1	Subdomain 2	Subdomain 3
Field	Career Growth	Work and Life	Fulfilling Work
Fun	Creative Pursuits	Travel	Storytelling
Faith	Core Beliefs	Spiritual Practices	Faith in Action
Future	Personal Growth	Skill Development	Goal Setting
Family	Family Relationships	Marriage	Parenting
Focus	Life Principles	Time Management	Resilience
Finances	Budgeting	Saving & Investing	Wealth Creation
Fellowship	Success Habits	Mentorship	Contribution

Fit Life	Healthy Eating	Exercise	Living Spaces
Foundations	Citizenship	Community	Economics
Friendship	Building	Networking	Navigating Change

If you really focus in and consider your story, it will fit into one of these 33 subdomains. The purpose of this specificity is clarity, to help your reader move forward in her life.

Yes, it will be tempting to want to touch on two, three, or maybe even ALL of these domains in your book. After all, this is your hope*story, and your story involves so many of these areas of life. But to truly write a book that helps a specific reader, let's get as specific as we possibly can.

Why Give Focus to Your Book's Problem

Before we specifically walk through each of these domains to help you discover the perfect subdomain for your book, let's first get clear on why it is so important to clarify the one problem your book addresses. There are three reasons to clearly articulate the problem—or the Y—of your book. First, the problem you address helps identify your book's category. That's right. Your book will be placed in a bookstore (either physically or digitally) one day. Isn't that exciting? So, in which section will your book be placed? What category will it live in? Your Y can give you that clarity.

Second, your Y helps define your industry. Yes, as an author, you are now part of an industry. For example, family/parenting advice is a different industry than field/career growth. An industry has conferences, media (such as podcasts and newsletters), and experts.

Finally, identifying your Y makes it easier for someone to know when they need to read your book. Your book fits into the story of their life at a specific moment in time. Consider the different challenges they experience in their various life stages and focus on one specific problem, concern, or obstacles. A married woman doesn't need dating advice, but she once did. A childless man doesn't need parenting advice, but he may someday. Clarifying the specific problem (the Y) that your target person (the X) is facing will help your reader gain the most benefit from the book you're writing.

Walking through the Domains

Taking all of the complexities of life and narrowing them down into only 11 areas was a herculean task. It's not a perfect system, but it will help you move forward. I've generally found that their most "hope stories" fit within one of these 11 domains of life and one of these 33 subdomains. Are there exceptions? Of course. But I'd encourage you to look for the connection to one specific subdomain. It may feel as though your story is like shoving a square peg into a round hole at first. But, what you'll discover is that the "square peg" of your story actually needs a bit of rounding, and a bit of editing to better tell the story!

Now, let's dive into the 11 domains of life and their subdomains.

As you read through these descriptions, pay special attention to the subdomains that resonate with you the most. You likely have something to say about most of these subdomains, but you'll find that there will be two or three that will stand out the most.

Choose Your Domain

Field

The **Field** domain focuses on professional life and career development. Consider writing about your career experiences and the lessons you've learned along the way.

- **Career Growth:** Share strategies for advancing in your career, including personal stories of success and the skills that helped you get there.
- **Work and Life Balance:** Offer insights on balancing career ambitions with personal life, drawing from your own experiences in maintaining harmony and fulfillment.
- **Fulfilling Work:** Write about finding purpose and satisfaction in your job, and how you turned your passion into a rewarding career.

Fun

The **Fun** domain is all about enriching life through joy, creativity, and adventure. Think about writing on topics that bring you happiness and encourage your imagination.

- **Creative Pursuits:** Inspire readers by sharing your creative hobbies, whether it's art, music, writing, or other forms of expression.
- **Travel:** Share your travel stories and tips, emphasizing the personal growth and joy that comes from exploring new places and cultures.
- **Storytelling:** Teach the art of storytelling by sharing how you craft compelling narratives, whether for personal enjoyment or professional endeavors.

Faith

The **Faith** domain explores spiritual growth and living out one's beliefs. Consider writing about your spiritual journey and how your faith shapes your life.

- **Core Beliefs:** Discuss the importance of understanding and solidifying your core beliefs, theology, and worldview and how they guide your decisions and actions.

- **Spiritual Practices:** Offer guidance on the spiritual practices that have strengthened your faith, from prayer and meditation to church attendence and more.

- **Faith in Action:** Show how you live out your faith in everyday life, and the impact of faith-driven actions on personal and community well-being.

Future

The **Future** domain focuses on personal development and preparing for what lies ahead. Write about your experiences in setting goals, acquiring new skills, and planning for a successful future.

- **Personal Growth:** Share your journey of self-improvement and personal development, providing tools and insights that helped you become your best self.

- **Skill Development:** Highlight the importance of continuous learning and skill acquisition, offering practical advice on developing new abilities.

- **Goal Setting:** Explain effective goal-setting techniques and share how you've achieved meaningful objectives in your life.

Family

The **Family** domain centers on nurturing strong family bonds and healthy relationships. Consider writing about your family experiences and the lessons you've learned.

- **Family Relationships:** Explore the dynamics of your family relationships, offering advice on building and maintaining strong, healthy connections with loved ones.

- **Marriage:** Provide insights into creating a successful and fulfilling marriage, addressing common challenges and how you overcame them.

- **Parenting:** Share strategies for effective parenting, covering topics from discipline to nurturing a child's development and well-being based on your own experiences.

Focus

The **Focus** domain emphasizes personal discipline and resilience. Write about the principles and practices that have helped you stay focused and resilient.

- **Life Principles:** Discuss the foundational principles that guide your life, encouraging readers to identify and live by their own set of values.

- **Time Management:** Offer practical tips for managing time effectively, sharing how you've balanced your responsibilities and priorities.

- **Resilience:** Teach the importance of resilience and how you've developed it, providing strategies for overcoming adversity and bouncing back stronger.

Finances

The **Finances** domain provides guidance on financial management and wealth building. Share your experiences and strategies for managing money and building wealth.

- **Budgeting:** Guide readers on how to create and stick to a budget, emphasizing the importance of financial discipline and planning from your own experiences.

- **Saving & Investing:** Explain the basics of saving and investing, helping readers secure their financial future with insights from your journey.

- **Wealth Creation:** Discuss strategies for creating wealth, from entrepreneurship to smart financial planning and investments, based on what you've learned.

Fellowship

The **Fellowship** domain focuses on building your own impact in your community of influence. Share your experiences with mentorship and contributing to your community.

- **Success Habits:** Highlight habits that have contributed to your success, offering practical advice on how to incorporate them into daily life.

- **Mentorship:** Explain the value of mentorship, both as a mentor and mentee and how you've cultivated these beneficial relationships.

- **Contribution:** Inspire readers to contribute to their communities and beyond, showing the impact of giving back and making a difference based on your experiences.

Fit Life

The **Fit Life** domain is dedicated to health and well-being. Write about your journey towards a healthier lifestyle, including tips on nutrition, exercise, and your home environment.

- **Nutrition:** Provide guidance on healthy eating habits, emphasizing the importance of diet in overall well-being from your perspective.

- **Exercise:** Offer tips and routines for maintaining physical fitness, sharing the benefits of regular exercise that you've experienced.

- **Living Spaces:** Discuss the impact of living spaces on health and productivity, offering advice on creating a positive and nurturing environment based on your experiences.

Foundations

The **Foundations** domain focuses on the deeper, more philosophical aspects of life that help readers better engage with and understand the world around them. Write about your experiences and insights on citizenship, community involvement, and economic awareness.

- **Citizenship:** Explore the responsibilities and benefits of being an engaged and active citizen, encouraging readers to contribute positively to society.

- **Community:** Discuss the importance of community involvement and how you've built and sustained strong community ties.

- **Economics:** Explain basic economic principles and their impact on personal and community life, helping readers understand and navigate the economic landscape based on your knowledge.

Friendship

The **Friendship** domain emphasizes the importance of social connections and adaptability. Share your experiences in building and maintaining friendships, networking, and handling changes in relationships.

- **Building:** Offer advice on building and maintaining strong, meaningful friendships, emphasizing the importance of social connections from your experiences.

- **Networking:** Teach effective networking strategies, helping readers expand their professional and personal circles with tips from your journey.

- **Navigating Change:** Provide guidance on the difficult areas of relationships, including setting boundaries, ending relationships, dealing with disappointment, offering strategies for maintaining stability, embracing your unique identity, and dealing with conflict in your relationships.

Now that we've walked through the 33 subdomains, it's your turn! Review the list and consider which areas of life are most intriguing and interesting to you. Where do you have the most powerful stories and deepest insights? Complete the following worksheet identifying your top two domains and then decide on the final choice for your book.

YOUR KEY DOMAINS AND SUBDOMAINS

1. **Domain:** _____

   Subdomain 1: _____

   Subdomain 2: _____

2. **Domain:** _____

   Subdomain 1: _____

   Subdomain 2: _____

3. **Final Choice Domain:** _____

   Subdomain 1: _____

   Subdomain 2: _____

REFLECTION

Why did you choose these domains and subdomains?

_____

_____

_____

_____

How do your experiences and insights align with these areas?

_____

_____

_____

_____

What unique perspectives or lessons can you share in these areas?

_____

_____

_____

_____

Use this worksheet to help you focus your writing efforts on the areas where you have the most passion and knowledge. This will make your book more engaging and impactful for your readers.

Z: Defining the Promise You Offer

The final part of the XYZ statement is the "Z"—the promise or solution your story provides. This is the transformation your readers can expect after reading your book. To define this promise, consider what thriving looks like in your chosen subdomain. Reflect on the challenges you overcame and the lessons you learned. What outcome do you want your readers to achieve? What new insight do you want them to have?

When crafting your "Z," think about the specific positive outcomes your story offers. The promise you offer should resonate with your audience and provide a clear path to the "promised land" you envision for them.

Your "Z" is the promise that keeps readers turning the pages and finding value in your story. By clearly articulating this promise, you ensure that your book delivers a meaningful message to inspire and guide your readers toward overcoming their challenges.

As you think through the promise you want to share in your story, consider the "before" and "after" in the specific subdomain of life you are addressing. Reflect on what it looked like for you to struggle. What were the challenges and obstacles you faced? How did these difficulties affect your daily life, mindset, and overall well-being? By painting a vivid picture of the struggle you faced or overcame, you help your readers connect with your story and apply your insights to their lives.

Defining Your Promise and Transformation

Instructions: Use this worksheet to think through the promise you want to share in your story. Reflect on the "before" and "after" states in the specific subdomain of life you are addressing. This will help you clearly define the transformation you want your readers to experience.

1. **Subdomain of Life:**

   (e.g., Career Growth, Parenting, Healthy Eating)

   _____

2. **The Struggle (Before):**
   Describe the challenges you faced in this area:

   _____

   _____

   _____

   How did these challenges affect your daily life, mindset, and well-being?

   _____

   _____

   _____

3. **The Transformation (After):**
   What does it look like to thrive in this area?

   _____

   _____

   _____

   Describe the feelings of achievement, satisfaction, and joy that came with overcoming your struggles:

   _____

   _____

   _____

4. **Strategies and Lessons Learned:**

   What specific strategies or habits helped you overcome the challenges?

   _____

   _____

   _____

   What mindset shifts contributed to your transformation?

   _____

   _____

   _____

5. **Defining Your Promise:**

   What positive outcome or change does your story offer to readers?

   _____

   _____

   _____

   How can your experiences and lessons help guide your readers toward this positive change?

   _____

   _____

   _____

Example Promise Statements

Example 1:

This book will help you cultivate a financial plan like a thriving garden, where each step is designed to plant seeds of stability and growth. Just as you nurture your garden to bloom, you'll learn to tend to your finances with care and purpose. By following this approach, you'll gain peace of mind, knowing that your financial future is secure.

Example 2:

This book will guide you in building meaningful friendships through outdoor activities like hiking. By connecting your love for nature with the desire for community, you'll discover how to forge strong, lasting bonds with like-minded individuals. Through shared adventures and faith-based insights, you'll not only enjoy the great outdoors but also create a network of supportive friends who share your passion for health, wellness, and living life to the fullest.

Example 3:

This book will introduce you to the 'presence model,' a revolutionary approach to balancing your business and family life. By integrating your family into your business rather than seeing them as competing priorities, you'll discover how to be an involved parent while continuing to run a successful enterprise. Learn how to maximize the time you have and create a harmonious life where your business and family thrive together.

Summarize your promise in a clear, concise promise statement:

_____

_____

_____

_____

_____

Finalize your XYZ Statement

Now, let's bring it all together. You've clearly defined your ideal reader, the X in the XYZ statement. You've also identified your Y, the specific area of life you want to write about, and the problem your reader is facing in that area. Finally, you've clarified your Z, the promise you're offering by telling your story in your book. Let's put it all together on one page.

X: My ideal reader is . . .

_____

_____

_____

Y: The problem in the subdomain of life that I'm addressing in my book is . . .

_____

_____

_____

Z: The promise that my book is offering my reader to help her overcome her challenge is . . .

_____

_____

_____

Congratulations! You now have more clarity than 99% of first-time authors. You've decided to start with your people, being very specific about the person, the problem, and the promise your book offers. Now, it's time to craft a concise, memorable XYZ statement. Even though you've done great work so far, it's way too wordy! We need to use the least amount of words for the most impact. In the next section, I'll provide you with example XYZ statements. Using these examples and the work you've already done, I want you to narrow down and rewrite your X, Y, and Z to 10 words or less. Yes, that's a total of 30 words or less. Aim for between 25 to 30 words, as this is the ideal length for an XYZ statement.

Example XYZ Statements

Example 1:

> **X:** Busy stay-at-home moms
> **Y:** Overcome overwhelm and chaos
> **Z:** So they can create a peaceful and organized haven for their families.

Example 2:

> **X:** First-year classroom teachers
> **Y:** Overcome classroom management struggles
> **Z:** So they can confidently create a positive learning environment that nurtures students.

Example 3:

> **X:** Christian online entrepreneurs
> **Y:** Overcome fear of sharing their faith online
> **Z:** So they can impact lives with their message and build a community of believers.

Now it's your turn to create your XYZ Statement.

WORKSHEET: CRAFTING YOUR XYZ STATEMENT

Instructions: Use this worksheet to create your XYZ statement. Reflect on who your audience is, the problem they are facing, and the promise or transformation your book offers. This will help you clearly define the purpose and impact of your story.

_____

_____

_____

1. **Identifying Your Audience (X):**

   Who is your target audience?

   _____

   _____

   _____

   _____

   _____

2. **Defining the Problem (Y):**

   What specific problem or challenge is your audience facing?

   _____

   _____

   _____

   _____

   _____

3. **Articulating the Promise (Z):**

   What positive outcome or transformation does your book offer?

   _____

   _____

   _____

   _____

   _____

   _____

   _____

4. **Crafting Your XYZ Statement:**

   Combine your answers into a single XYZ statement:

   X: _____

   Y: _____

   Z: _____

Reflection:

Why is this XYZ statement important for your book?

   _____

   _____

   _____

   _____

   _____

   _____

Step 2: Your Transformation Tale

Now that you have a clear XYZ statement for your book, the next step is to map out the content you are going to write. We will create the roadmap for the story you will tell in your book, beginning with the problem, following a path, and leading to the promise. In other words, we will plan out how your book will take X (your reader) on a journey from Y (the problem), following a path (your process), to Z (the promise). We call this journey "The Transformation Tale."

The Transformation Tale is a different way to approach your book outline. Instead of starting with chapter names and numbers, it focuses on the steps for your reader to get from stuck to success. The Transformation Tale helps frame your story FOR the reader, providing an organized narrative structure they can follow as they read your book.

The book you are writing is a narrative non-fiction book. It's your story (narrative) that actually happened (non-fiction). The narrative is the storytelling part, and people love to read a good story. The non-fiction is the application part, where you share lessons learned and steps your reader can take in her life. When combined, you create a book that is not only engaging but also helps her move forward in a key domain of her life. So, how exactly do you do this? How do you structure a book that both engages and educates your reader? By having a clear process mapped out, following your Transformation Tale.

Here is the general structure of a transformation tale in a narrative non-fiction book:

1. **The Prison**: At the beginning of your book, describe where you were stuck in one subdomain of life. Tell your story. Share the challenge. Relate this to the current state of your reader's life. What is the prob-

lem she is currently facing? Where does she feel stuck right now? Articulating this problem clearly will help her trust you because you know what it's like to be stuck. You know what it feels like to face that problem, to feel stuck in the "prison" she is currently stuck in.

2. **The Path**: Most of the chapters in your book will walk your reader through your process of transformation, the path you walked from the prison to the promised land. This may be a series of empowering truths you learned to embrace or it could be the specific action steps you took to get unstuck and move toward a solution.

3. **The Promise**: The goal of your book is to help your reader change her life, to help her move towards a new level of freedom in a key domain of her life. With that being said, of course, your book should end with the promise of your process fulfilled! Clearly paint the picture of what is possible if she now takes action, implementing the steps you explained throughout your book.

Instead of randomly typing out your stories (like most first-time authors do), you are going to pause and reflect, creating a roadmap for your reader to follow. This will provide her with clarity, helping her see your story as a tool to guide her on her journey of transformation.

Creating a Transformation Tale that follows the "problem, path, promise" process has several advantages for both you and the reader. For the reader, it makes your book extremely accessible and readable, as it is clear where you are leading her throughout your book. For you, the writer, it makes your job easier, as it is your mission to walk her through your process of transformation by sharing your story to get her moving forward from stuck to success.

To help you create your own Transformation Tale, we'll walk through two exercises. First, the high-level overview. Then the more detailed step-by-step process.

Your Transformation Tale: Mapping Out Your Book

The Transformation Tale helps frame your story for the reader, providing a clearly organized narrative structure. Here's a step-by-step guide to outline your book using the Transformation Tale approach.

1. The Prison: Defining the Problem

Objective: Describe where you were stuck.

Current State: Relate this to the reader's current situation. What problem is she facing?

Empathy: Articulate the problem clearly to build trust. Show that you understand the struggle and the feeling of being stuck.

_____

_____

_____

_____

Example Questions:

What is the main issue causing the reader to feel trapped?

_____

_____

_____

_____

How does this problem affect her everyday life?

_____

_____

_____

_____

What emotions does she feel in this "stuck state"?

_____

_____

_____

_____

2. The Path: Describing the Journey

Objective: Guide the reader through the process of transformation.

Steps: Outline the steps that led you from the problem to the solution.

Truths: Include the lessons, truths, or principles that were crucial in the transformation.

Action: Provide specific actions the reader can take to move toward a solution.

_____

_____

_____

_____

Example Questions:

What were the critical turning points in your journey?

_____

_____

_____

_____

What actions or changes had the most significant impact?

_____

_____

_____

_____

What mindset shifts or realizations were necessary?

_____

_____

_____

_____

3. The Promise: Declare the Future

Objective: Illustrate the potential outcome and new level of freedom.

Future State: Clearly depict what is possible if the reader takes action.

Benefits: Highlight the benefits and positive changes that will come from following the path.

Encouragement: Motivate the reader to take the steps outlined and assure them of the possibility of change.

_____

_____

_____

_____

Example Questions:

What does the transformed life look like?

_____

_____

_____

_____

How will solving the problem impact the reader's overall well-being?

_____

_____

_____

_____

What encouragement can you offer to inspire action?

_____

_____

_____

_____

Getting specific

Now that you have the general outline of your transformation tale, it's time to get very specific. What steps did you take to move from the prison to the promise?

Let's look at a clear example to help you see the transformation tale in action. The book is called *Again I Rise: Life After Divorce* by Sarah Author.

Here is her XYZ Statement:

X= A recently divorced, childless woman in her mid-thirties.

Y= Suffers from depression and lack of direction after the rejection of divorce.

Z= Moves to a new city and begins again with a new job and friend group.

Domain: Focus

Subdomain: Resilience

Transformation Tale:

1. Problem: The day he left.
2. Step 1: Awareness
3. Step 2: Seeking Support
4. Step 3: Self-Discovery
5. Step 4: Setting Goals
6. Step 5: The Big Move
7. Step 6: Overcoming Obstacles
8. Step 7: Embracing Change
9. Promise: The New World

This is an example you can follow and apply to your own story of transformation.

A *Clear Roadmap from Problem to Promise*

The Transformation Tale generally follows a nine-chapter structure. Here's how to break it down:

1. **Chapter One: The Problem She's Facing**

   ◦ Start by vividly describing the problem your reader is dealing with. Capture the emotions, struggles, and frustrations she experiences. This sets the stage and helps your reader see that you understand her plight.

   ◦ Example: "In the midst of a painful divorce, Sarah felt like she was drowning. Every day was a struggle to find a reason to get out of bed. She was overwhelmed by loneliness, fear, and uncertainty about the future."

2. **Chapters Two to Eight: The Steps in the Journey**

   ◦ Each middle chapter articulates a step in the journey from the problem to the promised land. Whether your journey includes five, seven, nine, or even ten steps, each step should be a chapter that provides clear guidance, insights, and practical actions your reader can take.

   ◦ For example, if the journey consists of seven steps:

Chapter Two: Awareness

- Discuss the importance of acknowledging the reality of the situation. Awareness is the first step towards healing and transformation.

- Example: "Sarah had to come to terms with her new reality. Awareness didn't mean giving up, but rather acknowledging the pain and allowing herself to start the healing process."

Chapter Three: Seeking Support

- Emphasize the value of finding a support system. Whether it's friends, family, or a support group, having others to lean on is crucial.

- Example: "Sarah reached out to a local support group for divorced women. Connecting with others who understood her pain provided her with much-needed comfort and encouragement."

Chapter Four: Self-Discovery

- Encourage self-reflection and exploration. Help your reader rediscover her strengths, passions, and values.

- Example: "Through journaling and personal reflection, Sarah began to rediscover her passions. She found solace in painting, something she had loved but neglected for years."

Chapter Five: Setting Goals

- Guide your reader in setting realistic and meaningful goals. Goals provide direction and a sense of purpose.

- Example: "Sarah set small, achievable goals for herself, such as exercising three times a week and reading a new book each month. These goals gave her a sense of accomplishment and progress."

Chapter Six: The Big Move

- Highlight the importance of taking concrete steps towards those goals. Action brings about change.

- Example: "Sarah decides to move and takes a job in a new city. She also joins a local church and connects to a new community. These activities not only helped her achieve her goals but also brought new friendships and joy into her life."

Chapter Seven: Overcoming Obstacles

- Address the inevitable challenges and setbacks. Provide strategies for overcoming obstacles and staying motivated.

- Example: "There were days when Sarah felt like giving up, but she reminded herself of how far she had come. She learned to be gentle with herself and seek help when needed."

Chapter Eight: Embracing Change

- Discuss the importance of embracing change and being open to new opportunities. Transformation requires a willingness to adapt.

- Example: "As Sarah embraced the changes in her life, she found new opportunities for growth and happiness. She learned to view change not as a threat, but as a chance to rise again."

3. **Chapter Nine: The Promised Land She Can Live In**

   ○ Paint a picture of the desired outcome—the promised land. Show what life can look like once she overcomes her challenges. This vision gives your reader hope and motivation to embark on the journey.

- ◦ Example: "Today, Sarah wakes up with a sense of purpose and joy. She has rebuilt her life, discovered her inner strength, and is living a life full of hope, surrounded by love and support. She has found peace and happiness that she never thought possible."

Each middle chapter articulates a step in the journey from the problem to the promised land. Whether your journey incluBy structuring your Transformation Tale in this way, you provide a clear and actionable path for your reader to follow. Each chapter builds on the previous one, guiding her step by step from the problem to the promised land.

Defining the steps

Now that you have a clear example of Sarah's book to follow, let's focus on helping you define your process. Your process is the step-by-step journey from the problem to the promise. The clearer you are about your process, the kinder it is for the reader. It's true that most progress in life is not linear; it can often feel like a meandering, accidental journey. However, looking back on your life experience, you can generally identify and describe phases or stages. These are the steps you can outline for your reader.

If you're struggling to see how your journey could serve as a roadmap for her journey, I have some encouragement for you. Your process doesn't have to be prescriptive; it can be descriptive. In other words, you're not telling her what to do in her life; you're sharing the story of what you did in yours. By reading your story, she will be encouraged to take action.

Where most writers get stuck is the specific steps the reader needs to take to move forward. To help you even more, here are a few exercises to help.

Here's what we're going to do next. First, I will walk you through a life-mapping exercise. This will help you look back on your journey from the problem to the promise and begin to identify the path you followed. Then I'll show you my favorite strategy for taking your story and turning it into a foundational framework that you can share on podcasts, teach from the stage, and, of course, use as the table of contents for your book. I call this the Foundational Framework.

LIFE MAPPING EXERCISE

Step One:

Let's start with where you were stuck. Vividly describe the problem that you faced. What was the specific date? Where were you living? What exactly happened? How did you feel? Describe any other details.

_____

_____

_____

_____

Step Two:

What happened next?

_____

_____

_____

_____

What was the first step you took?

_____

_____

_____

_____

What was the epiphany that you had?

_____

_____

_____

_____

What action did you take?

_____

_____

_____

_____

What was the result? What did that lead to?

_____

_____

_____

_____

Keep going with each of the steps in the journey until you reach the promise.

_____

_____

_____

_____

This life-mapping exercise can often be very delicate. It involves taking time to look back and consider your own journey. It's important to acknowledge that sometimes we need additional help. At hope*writers, we have an incredible team of writing coaches who can help you with this process. Just visit hopewriters.com/coaches to learn more. You might also consider sharing your journey with a friend, pastor, or counselor. Especially if you have a particularly hard story, it's important not to walk it alone.

The Foundational Framework

If you go back and trace the steps in your journey from the prison to the promise, you'll discover that you've developed "your way," a road map that other people can follow. It's worth taking some time to consider how this process can be honed and refined as your own system that you can teach and share with others. I call this process your "Foundational Framework."

An advanced strategy is to name this process with an acrostic. To help you create your Foundational Framework, I've provided three examples below. One for a book helping someone experience healing from trauma using the acrostic "HEALING," another for guiding a skeptic to a passionate belief in the God of the Bible using the acrostic "BELIEF," and a third for assisting overwhelmed first-year teachers in becoming confident veteran educators using the acrostic "TEACHER." Each acrostic serves as a step-by-step guide, offering a structured approach to overcoming challenges and achieving significant personal growth.

Example 1: Framework "HEALING" Related to Trauma

Here is an example using the acrostic "HEALING," which is designed to guide someone through the process of healing from childhood trauma. Each letter in "HEALING" represents a critical step in the journey from pain to recovery. By breaking down the transformation into Honesty, Empathy, Acceptance, Learning, Integration, Nurturing, and Growth, this acrostic offers a clear and structured path to follow.

Explanation of Each Step:

H - Honesty

- **Objective:** Acknowledge and confront the trauma.

- **Actions:** Journal about your experiences, talk to a trusted friend or therapist, and admit to yourself the reality of your past.

E - Empathy

- **Objective:** Show compassion to yourself.

- **Actions:** Practice self-compassion exercises, speak kindly to yourself, and give yourself permission to feel your emotions.

A - Acceptance

- **Objective:** Accept your past without letting it define you.

- **Actions:** Engage in acceptance and commitment therapy (ACT) exercises, and remind yourself that your past does not dictate your future.

L - Learning

- **Objective:** Educate yourself about trauma and its effects.

- **Actions:** Read books on trauma recovery, attend workshops or support groups, and stay informed about how trauma impacts the brain and body.

I - Integration

- **Objective:** Integrate new coping mechanisms and positive habits.

- **Actions:** Practice mindfulness, establish a regular meditation routine, and incorporate healthy lifestyle choices.

N - Nurturing

- **Objective:** Take care of your physical, emotional, and mental well-being.
- **Actions:** Develop a self-care routine and build a support network of friends and family.

G - Growth

- **Objective:** Embrace the journey of personal growth and transformation.
- **Actions:** Set personal growth goals, celebrate small victories, and stay committed to your healing journey.

Example 2: Framework "BELIEF" Moving from Skepticism to Faith

Here is an example using the acrostic "BELIEF," which is designed to guide someone from skepticism to a passionate belief in the God of the Bible. Each letter in "BELIEF" represents a crucial step in the journey from doubt to faith. By breaking down the transformation into Begin with Questions, Examine Evidence, Listen to Others, Invite God In, Experience Transformation, and Foster Growth, this acrostic offers a clear and structured path to follow:

B - Begin with Questions

- **Objective:** Acknowledge and explore your doubts.
- **Actions:** Write down your questions, read books by authors who have explored similar doubts, and discuss your questions with trusted friends or mentors.

E - Examine Evidence

- **Objective:** Investigate the historical, philosophical, and personal evidence for the God of the Bible.
- **Actions:** Study apologetic resources, attend lectures or debates on the existence of God, and read the Bible with an open mind.

L - Listen to Others

- **Objective:** Engage with people who have a strong faith.
- **Actions:** Join a faith-based discussion group, listen to podcasts or sermons, and ask believers about their personal experiences with God.

I - Invite God In

- **Objective:** Open your heart to the possibility of God's existence.
- **Actions:** Spend time in prayer, asking God to reveal Himself to you, and attend church services to experience worship and community.

E - Experience Transformation

- **Objective:** Allow your faith to start influencing your life.
- **Actions:** Reflect on changes in your life as you begin to believe, journal about your experiences, and start incorporating faith-based practices into your daily routine.

F - Foster Growth

- **Objective:** Nurture your new faith by immersing yourself in a faith community and continually seeking a deeper relationship with God.

- **Actions:** Regularly attend church, join a Bible study group, read the Bible daily, and continue to seek mentorship and guidance in your faith journey.

Example 3: Framework "TEACHER" Becoming a Confident Teacher

Here is a third example using the acrostic "TEACHER," which is designed to guide someone from being an overwhelmed first-year classroom teacher to a confident veteran educator changing students' lives. Each letter in "TEACHER" represents a crucial step in the journey from inexperience to expertise. By breaking down the transformation into Trust the Process, Engage with Students, Adapt and Innovate, Collaborate with Colleagues, Hone Your Skills, Evaluate and Reflect, and Renew Your Passion, this acrostic offers a clear and structured path to follow. This example demonstrates how you can use an acrostic to organize your thoughts and provide a comprehensive guide for your readers:

T - Trust the Process

- **Objective:** Understand that becoming an effective teacher is a journey.
- **Actions:** Embrace a growth mindset, be patient with yourself, and celebrate small victories along the way.

E - Engage with Students

- **Objective:** Build strong relationships with your students.
- **Actions:** Get to know your students individually, create a welcoming classroom environment, and use student interests to make learning relevant.

A - Adapt and Innovate

- **Objective:** Be flexible and open to new teaching methods and technologies.

- **Actions:** Experiment with different teaching techniques, integrate technology into your lessons, and personalize learning experiences.

C - Collaborate with Colleagues

- **Objective:** Seek support and advice from experienced teachers.

- **Actions:** Join professional learning communities, attend staff meetings, and seek mentorship from veteran teachers.

H - Hone Your Skills

- **Objective:** Continuously improve your teaching skills through professional development.

- **Actions:** Attend educational workshops and conferences, take courses, and read books and articles on effective teaching practices.

E - Evaluate and Reflect

- **Objective:** Regularly assess your teaching methods and their effectiveness.

- **Actions:** Collect and analyze student feedback, reflect on lesson outcomes, and adjust your teaching strategies as needed.

R - Renew Your Passion

- **Objective:** Maintain your enthusiasm for teaching.

- **Actions:** Set personal and professional goals, find a work-life balance, celebrate student successes, and stay connected to your reasons for becoming a teacher.

Now It's Your Turn

Consider the journey you've walked from the prison to the promise. Reflect on the steps you took to transform your life and overcome the challenges you faced. Now, come up with your own acrostic to help guide readers through their journey of transformation. Here are some tips to get you started:

1. **Reflect on Your Journey:**
   - Think about the significant milestones and turning points in your transformation.
   - Identify the key actions, mindsets, or principles that helped you move forward.

2. **Choose a Meaningful Word:**
   - Select a word that encapsulates the essence of your transformation.
   - Ensure that each letter of the word can represent a specific step or principle.

3. **Define Each Step:**
   - Clearly articulate what each letter stands for.
   - Provide detailed explanations, actions, and examples for each step.

WORKSHEET: NAMING YOUR PROCESS

Instructions:

Reflect on your journey from the prison to the promise. Consider the steps you took to transform your life and how you can turn this into a roadmap for others. Use the following prompts to create your own Foundational Framework and name it with an acrostic.

Your Foundational Framework Acrostic

1. **Choose a Meaningful Word**: Select a word that encapsulates the essence of your transformation. Ensure each letter of the word can represent a specific step or principle.

   Your Acrostic Word: _____

   _____

2. **Define Each Step**: Clearly articulate what each letter stands for. Provide detailed explanations, actions, and examples for each step.

Step-by-Step Guide

<u>Step 1</u>:

   Letter:

   _____

   _____

   Overview:

   _____

   _____

Objective:

_____

_____

Actions:

_____

_____

_____

_____

<u>Step 2</u>:

Letter:

_____

_____

Overview:

_____

_____

Objective:

_____

_____

Actions:

_____

_____

Step 3:

Letter:

_____

_____

Overview:

_____

_____

Objective:

_____

_____

Actions:

_____

_____

Step 4:

Letter:

_____

_____

Overview:

_____

_____

Objective:

_____

_____

Actions:

_____

_____

Step 5:

Letter:

_____

_____

Overview:

_____

_____

Objective:

_____

_____

Actions:

_____

_____

Step 6:

Letter:

_____

_____

Overview:

_____

_____

Objective:

_____

_____

Actions:

_____

_____

<u>Step 7:</u>

Letter:

_____

_____

Overview:

_____

_____

Objective:

_____

_____

Actions:

_____

_____

At this point in the journey, you're either feeling really encouraged because you figured out your Foundational Framework or a bit overwhelmed. Either way, I have some encouragement for you.

First, understand that developing your Foundational Framework is a process that takes time and may require multiple attempts to get it right. It can sometimes take a while to figure it out! Second, I found it helpful to share your journey on social media to get encouragement and feedback from others. Share parts of your story and continue to refine your foundational framework based on the feedback you receive.

Number three, not every story fits perfectly into a beautifully designed framework. That's OK! Following a logical sequence that encourages your reader to move from the problem to the promise is a clear and kind way to structure your book. It doesn't have to be perfect to help somebody else.

Step 3: Detailed Chapter Outlines

Now that we have clearly identified your XYZ statement and your Transformation Tale, it's time to create a detailed outline of each of the chapters in your book. This is the blueprint for your book. Where you create the overall plan for each chapter. In this section, I'll show you the different chapter elements that are commonly found in narrative nonfiction books, and I'll guide you through the process of deciding which of these elements to use in each of the chapters. The outcome of this section is that you will have the most comprehensive blueprint for your book which will serve as a companion as you begin to actually write your chapters. Let's get started. The detailed chapter outline provides a clear structure and plan for your book, ensuring that each chapter flows logically and effectively conveys your message.

Elements of a Chapter

In nonfiction writing, chapters are composed of specific elements that can help convey your message to your reader. These are the building blocks you can choose from to help build your chapters. Let's examine the 12 most used chapter elements.

A. Inspirational Quote

Description: Often, what you're saying in your chapter has been said before by someone who has spent a lifetime researching the topic or has developed a robust career. Including a quote from a respected figure (e.g., Jesus, Einstein, a well-known industry leader) helps frame the conversation and provides a memorable hook for the reader.

Purpose: Sets the tone for the chapter, provides authority, and connects your points to a broader context.

B. Intriguing Story

Description: Use an intriguing story that builds curiosity and draws the reader into the narrative. Stories often begin with drama or intrigue and include a hook that compels the reader to continue.

Purpose: Engages the reader emotionally, provides context, and illustrates key points.

C. Teaching Section

Description: Begin with a thesis statement that identifies the main point, followed by three to five supporting points, and conclude with a summary.

Purpose: Clearly communicates the main ideas and supporting arguments, making the content accessible and understandable.

D. Citing Research

Description: Include market research, data, and statistics, either publicly available or from your own surveys. Start with the main problem or finding and break it down into key points or statistics.

Purpose: Provides evidence and credibility to support your arguments and insights.

E. Limits and Truths

Description: This three-step structure involves identifying a past limiting belief, describing the experience or realization that challenged it, and sharing the new empowering truth.

Purpose: Demonstrates personal growth and transformation, encouraging the reader to adopt new perspectives.

F. Historical Context

Description: Share the story of a historical character, their desires, experiences, and lessons, relating it to the chapter's theme.

Purpose: Offers a broader perspective and connects the chapter's content to historical events and figures.

G. Relatable Client Anecdotes

Description: Reference other clients, social media followers, or friends who have faced similar resistance or hesitation. Telling their stories helps the reader see themselves in these characters and opens the possibility for transformation.

Purpose: Provides relatable examples and demonstrates real-life applications of the chapter's concepts.

H. Visual Aids

Description: Include diagrams, charts, or images that illustrate key points.

Purpose: Enhances understanding and retention of information through visual representation.

I. Personal Reflection

Description: Share personal experiences related to the chapter's topic.

Purpose: Builds a personal connection with the reader and provides authenticity.

J. Practical Exercises

Description: Include step-by-step activities or exercises that the reader can do to apply the chapter's teachings.

Purpose: Encourages active participation and helps the reader implement the concepts.

K. Journal Prompts

Description: Invite the reader to pause and reflect on what they've learned in the chapter with guided questions.

Purpose: Encourages deeper engagement and personal application of the chapter's content.

L. Discussion Questions

Description: Provide questions for the reader to discuss the content with another person.

Purpose: Facilitates deeper understanding through conversation and collaboration.

Analyzing Chapter Structures

Before we identify the elements you will include in your chapters, I have a powerful exercise to share that has helped our published authors elevate their books to a world-class level. This exercise involves examining comparable books before structuring your own. In most areas of life, I've come to understand that success leaves clues. When we take the time to study someone else's work and investigate how they've structured it, it will better inform our own work. Here's the process:

1. Begin with your subdomain. If you've been following along, you've already identified your subdomain out of the 33 options.

2. Browse The Hope 100. At our hope*books store, we carry a curated selection of life-changing books recommended by our community, categorized into the subdomains of life. This collection is called the Hope

100. You can access it by visiting thehope100.com. Find your subdomain and the three recommended books in that area.

3. Purchase or borrow these books from the library. Then, examine the chapter structure they follow in their book. For example, the chapters might start with an inspirational quote, then a personal story, followed by citing research, a verse from scripture, journal prompt questions, and finally, personal reflection.

Elements:

A. Inspirational Quote	B. Intriguing Story	C. Teaching Section
D. Citing Research	E. Limits and Truths	F. Historical Context
G. Client Anecdotes	H. Visual Aids	I. Personal Reflection
J. Practical Exercises	K. Journal Prompts	L. Discussion Questions

Example:

Book Title: *Again I Rise: Life After Divorce*
Author Name: Sarah Author
Chapter Number and Name: Chapter 5: Setting Goals
    Element One: A. Inspirational Quote
    Element Two: B. Intriguing Story
    Element Three: D. Citing Research
    Element Four: C. Teaching Section
    Element Five: H. Visual Aids
    Element Six: J. Practical Exercises
    Element Seven: I. Personal Reflection

Now it's your turn!

Exercise One: Book #1

Book Title:

_____

_____

Author Name:

_____

_____

Chapter Number and Name:

_____

_____

    Element One:

    _____

    _____

    Element Two:

    _____

    _____

    Element Three:

    _____

    _____

    Element Four:

    _____

    _____

    Element Five:

    _____

    _____

Element Six:

_____

_____

Element Seven:

_____

_____

Exercise Two: Book #2

Book Title:

_____

_____

Author Name:

_____

_____

Chapter Number and Name:

_____

_____

Element One:

_____

_____

Element Two:

_____

_____

Element Three:

_____

_____

Element Four:

_____

_____

Element Five:

_____

_____

Element Six:

_____

_____

Element Seven:

_____

_____

Exercise Three: Book #3

Book Title:

_____

_____

Author Name:

_____

_____

Chapter Number and Name:

_____

_____

Element One:

_____

_____

Element Two:

_____

_____

Element Three:

_____

_____

Element Four:

_____

_____

Element Five:

_____

_____

Element Six:

_____

_____

Element Seven:

_____

_____

Summarize each of your three model books below:

Here is an example summary for _Again I Rise: Life After Divorce_ by Sarah Author: A, B, D, C, E, J, I

Here it is all typed out: (A) Inspirational Quote, (B) Intriguing Story, (D) Citing Research, (C)Teaching Section, (E) Limits and Truths, (J) Practical Exercises, (I) Personal Reflection

Book One:

_____

_____

_____

Book Two:

_____

_____

_____

Book Three:

_____

_____

_____

Use the template above to outline each chapter in your book. This approach will ensure that your chapters are well-structured and provide a consistent, enjoyable reading experience for your audience.

WORKSHEET: CREATING YOUR OWN BLUEPRINT

Once you have analyzed the structure of chapters from three different books, you can start to outline your own chapters using the patterns you've identified. Here's a suggested template based on common structures:

Chapter Title: Choose a title that captures the essence of the chapter.

_____

_____

A. **Inspirational Quote**: Begin with a relevant quote that sets the tone for the chapter and aligns with the chapter's theme.

_____

_____

_____

_____

B. **Intriguing Story:** Share a personal story or anecdote that introduces the topic.

_____

_____

_____

_____

C. **Teaching Section:**

    a. Describe the first key point or lesson.

    _____

_____

_____

_____

b. **Point Two:** Discuss the second key point or lesson.

_____

_____

_____

_____

c. **Point Three:** Elaborate on the third key point or lesson.

_____

_____

_____

_____

D. **Citing Research:** Include relevant data or statistics to support your points.

_____

_____

_____

_____

E. **Historical Context:** Share relevant historical anecdotes that support the chapter's theme.

_____

_____

_____

_____

F. **Limits and Truths:** Share a belief you once held.

_____

_____

_____

_____

G. **Client Anecdotes:** Provide stories of clients or followers who have faced similar challenges and transformations.

_____

_____

_____

_____

H. **Personal Reflection:** Summarize the key points and provide a closing thought.

_____

_____

_____

_____

I. **Journal Prompts:** Include prompts that encourage the reader to reflect on the chapter's content.

_____

_____

_____

_____

J. **Discussion Questions:** End with questions that encourage the reader to discuss the content with others.

_____

_____

_____

_____

Over the last several pages, you've outlined the elements for each chapter of your book. You now know exactly which elements you will be utilizing in every chapter. This detailed chapter outline will serve as a clear blueprint as we move toward writing your book. If this process has become stuck or feels overwhelming, we've created a video tutorial to walk you through it. Visit hopebooks.com/dco for a step-by-step guide on the detailed chapter outline process.

Step 4: Writing Your Model Chapter

And now onto the fun part. It's time to actually start writing. We're not going to begin writing your book from start to finish just yet. Instead, we'll focus on one model chapter. This will give you a chance to flesh out your content following your detailed chapter outline. It will also provide assurance that you've chosen the right elements or reveal whether you need to make adjustments before continuing with the rest of your book.

One of the biggest mistakes that first-time authors make is starting their book by randomly writing without a clear structure. This often leads to a jumbled mess of words that feels unstructured, unclear, and unorganized. At hope*books, we teach a clearly structured process for getting your story out of your head and heart and onto the page in a well-crafted and engaging way. This step-by-step approach gives you the courage and confidence to continue sharing your story, ensuring it's well-written and impactful.

Steps to Write Your Model Chapter

Step 1: Draft Out Your Chapter Elements

In the last section, you organized your detailed chapter outlines by selecting the order of your chapter elements. Now it's time to flesh out the content for these sections. If, for example, you use element A, Inspiring Quote, now it's time to find that quote and copy and paste it into your document. If you include element B. Intriguing Story, it's time to write out the draft of that story.

Step 2: Follow the Three-Step Writing Process

In her fantastic book on writing, *Bird by Bird*, Anne Lamott, describes a three-step writing process that I recommend all of our authors follow. These three steps include the Down Draft, the Up Draft, and the Dental Draft. This method ensures a thorough and organized writing process.

- **Down Draft: Get It Down**
  - The Down Draft is the first draft, where you get all your thoughts out of your head and heart and onto the page. It can be messy, but that's okay. The goal is to get everything down so you can work with it. The key here is to write without worrying about grammar, structure, or perfection. Focus on capturing your ideas and stories.

- **Up Draft: Clean It Up**
  - The Up Draft is the second draft, where you clean up your words. This step involves cutting out unnecessary sections, adding new ones, combining stories, and refining your content. The key here is to review your initial draft, make necessary changes, and enhance clarity and coherence.

- **Dental Draft: Polish and Perfect**
  - The Dental Draft is the final draft, where you edit your writing meticulously. This step might involve having someone else review your work. At hope*books, we recommend using a developmental editor to provide feedback and suggestions for improvement. The key here is to focus on grammar, punctuation, and fine-tuning your narrative.

Writing a model chapter is a crucial step that will set the tone and structure for the rest of your book. By following this process, you ensure that each chapter is well-crafted, engaging, and consistent. This structured approach makes the writing process more manageable and helps you complete the writing of your book in record time.

Workbook Exercise: Writing Your Model Chapter

Exercise Overview:

1. **Select Your Elements:**
   - Review the list of chapter elements and choose which ones you'll include in your model chapter.

2. **Down Draft:**
   - Write your initial draft, getting all your ideas down without worrying about perfection.

3. **Up Draft:**
   - Refine your draft by cutting unnecessary sections, adding new ones, and ensuring your narrative flows smoothly.

4. **Dental Draft:**
   - Polish your draft, focusing on grammar, punctuation, and fine-tuning. Consider having a developmental editor review your work.

After you finish your detailed chapter outline, it's time to write your model chapter. We start with one chapter that can serve as the perfect example for the other 9 to 12 chapters you'll include in your book. First, write it down, then clean it up, and finally, go line by line and word by word.

I highly recommend that you, as the author, take care of the first two steps: you write it down and clean it up. However, it's important to have someone else edit your words. As the author, it's often difficult to edit your own work because you are the one who wrote the words. There is often a gap between the voice we hear inside our heads and the words we type on the screen.

At hope*books, this is where we have a developmental editor review your chapter. This objective professional can review your work and give you feedback, helping you polish your content to better convey your message to your reader. Later in this book, we will cover the three different ways to publish. Whether you choose traditional publishing, self-publishing, or Hope Publishing, I highly recommend having an editor review your work and help you create the best model chapter possible before continuing to write the rest of the book. This will help set a standard to follow as you finish your manuscript.

Step 5: Write Your Manuscript

Now that you have your entire blueprint, including your detailed chapter outline and model chapter, it's time to finish your book. This can be the part that feels overwhelming and holds a lot of people back, but with the right approach and mindset, you can do it. Below are some tips I've gleaned from our guest teachers at hope*writers over the years. To get a free trial of hope*writers, just go to hopewriters.com/try.

Here's how to actually write your whole manuscript:

1. **Begin with the End in Mind** Set a clear date for finishing your manuscript. At hope*books, we recommend 60 days. So, take out your calendar right now, or ask your favorite personal assistant, Alexa or Siri, what the date is 60 days from now. Mark that date as your manuscript completion goal.

2. **Put It on the Calendar** Break down your writing task into manageable chunks. If your book has 12 chapters, plan to write one chapter per week for the next 12 weeks if your goal is to finish in 90 days. If you aim to finish in 60 days, plan to write one chapter every five days. Write this schedule down and put it on your calendar. A calendar is the tool of professionals, and you are a professional.

The key here is to make an appointment with yourself. On a high level, determine which chapter you will finish by when. Then, look at your daily schedule and identify the chunks of time and cracks of time you will dedicate to writing.

Introducing Chunk Time and Crack Time

Chunk Time: This is when you can dedicate an hour or more to writing. This might mean taking several days off to go to your lake house or simply finding an hour after dropping the kids off at school. Plan for these larger blocks of time and protect them.

Crack Time: Sometimes, the little 10- to 15-minute segments in our day are even more effective than the chunk time. These are the moments between appointments while waiting, driving, or walking.

Example Writing Schedules:

15-Hour Writing Week:

- Monday: 2 hours in the morning, 1 hour in the evening
- Tuesday: 1 hour in the morning, 1 hour in the afternoon
- Wednesday: 2 hours in the morning, 1 hour in the evening
- Thursday: 1 hour in the morning, 1 hour in the afternoon
- Friday: 2 hours in the morning, 1 hour in the evening
- Saturday: 2 hours in the afternoon

8-Hour Writing Week:

- Monday: 1 hour in the morning, 1 hour in the evening
- Tuesday: 1 hour in the morning
- Wednesday: 1 hour in the evening
- Thursday: 1 hour in the morning, 1 hour in the evening

- Friday: 1 hour in the afternoon
- Saturday: 1 hour in the afternoon

3-Hour Writing Week:

- Monday: 30 minutes in the morning, 30 minutes in the evening
- Wednesday: 1 hour in the evening
- Friday: 1 hour in the afternoon

3. **Implementing Your Writing Plan** Once you've set your schedule, stick to it. Treat these writing times as sacred appointments with yourself. You are not just writing a book; you are fulfilling a mission, sharing your story, and making an impact.

Writing a manuscript can feel like running a marathon. There will be times when enthusiasm wanes, but having a clear plan and structure will keep you moving forward. By breaking your task into manageable pieces and sticking to your schedule, you will find the process more enjoyable and achievable. Keep your end goal in sight, and know that each writing session brings you one step closer to sharing your story with the world.

How to Use Your Detailed Chapter Outline

Now that you have your detailed chapter outline, it's time to put it to good use. The key is to always have your book with you so you can make the most of your available time, especially those little pockets of time. Here's how to do it:

Print Out Your Detailed Chapter Outline

- Print a copy of your detailed chapter outline and keep it with you at all times. Having a tangible copy allows you to quickly reference your next section and work on it whenever you have a spare moment.

Make the Most of Crack Time

- Utilize those 10- to 15-minute segments in your day—while commuting, waiting, or during breaks. Your printed outline will serve as a constant reminder of your progress and what you need to write next.

Three Ways to Actually Write It Down

One of the biggest challenges all writers face is sitting down and writing the manuscript of their book. We've set you up for success since at this point, all you need to do is follow your detailed chapter outline. But how do you actually get your words out of your head and onto the screen? In other words, how do you get your words down?

Three techniques have worked for thousands of our members at hope*writers and me. First, you can use a voice recording app to speak your words out loud. Second, you can record a conversation with a friend. And third, you can sit down and write it out. Let's explore each of these options to find the one that is right for you.

1. Talk It Out

Many of us spend a significant amount of time in the car commuting to work, driving kids to school, or running errands. This is unclaimed writing time that you can harness effectively. Imagine having a piece of paper on your dashboard with the next section you need to write. Here's how to use voice recording to capture your thoughts:

How to Do It:

- **Step 1:** Identify the next section you need to write from your outline. For example, let's say you need to tell the introductory story for Chapter 7 about the power of your 7th-grade English teacher who believed in you.

- **Step 2:** Take out your phone, open the voice memos app, and press record. Start by explaining what you're going to talk about. For instance, "Today I'm going to record the story about how my 7th-grade English teacher believed in me."

- **Step 3:** Just start talking. Tell the story in full detail. If you miss something, keep going and add it in later. The most important thing is to keep talking.

Example: "When I was in 7th grade, I had an English teacher named Mrs. Johnson who believed in me. She saw potential in my writing and encouraged me to enter a school essay competition. I remember how she took the time to help me refine my ideas and build my confidence. This experience taught me the power of belief and support in shaping one's future."

- **Step 4:** If you realize you missed a detail, just say, "I want to add a detail at the beginning," and then continue.

Once you've recorded your voice, you can always use a transcription service to type out the words into a draft manuscript.

2. Have a Conversation

If you've been struggling to write your book, what if you simply sat down with a friend over coffee and had her interview you about your book? Give her your detailed chapter outline and have her ask you questions about it. You can talk out your ideas and have them recorded with your voice memos app or even record the conversation over Zoom!

3. Write It Down

Yes, this is the hardest one, but you can just sit down and type out your manuscript. I want you to know that this method is more of a "marathon" than a sprint. It can take time to write out your manuscript, especially since the average length of a narrative nonfiction book is 55,000 words.

4. Follow Your Own Process.

After interviewing over 200 authors in our online membership, hope*writers, we've discovered that everyone has their own process for writing their books. And some of those tips and hacks are really strange! The point is that we all have our own process that works—you just have to discover it. So try a few different ways to write your book until you find the process that works for you. Then keep going until you get your book done!

Prepare your manuscript for publication

Once you have your entire manuscript written and cleaned up (the Down Draft and the Up Draft), it's time to get some help. That's right—I don't recommend editing your own writing. Instead, at hope*books, we have a three-step editing process to ensure your manuscript is polished and ready for publication.

1. **Developmental Editor:** This first step involves a thorough review of your manuscript's structure,

content, and flow. The developmental editor provides feedback on big-picture elements like plot, character development, and overall coherence.

2. **Copy Assistant:** Next, the copy assistant focuses on the finer details, such as grammar, punctuation, and sentence structure. This step ensures your writing is clear, concise, and error-free.

3. **Beta Readers:** Finally, beta readers provide a fresh perspective by reading your manuscript as your target audience would. They offer valuable insights and suggestions based on their reading experience.

Each step allows you to update your manuscript based on the feedback and suggestions. Once you've applied these changes and made your updates, it's time to look at your publishing options, which we'll cover in the next section.

HOW TO GET YOUR STORY PUBLISHED

Now that you have more clarity about why and how to write your book, it's time to think about publishing. Publishing is the entire process of converting your typed manuscript into a printed book. There are many steps involved, which we will outline here, but the focus is the end goal. The end goal is to have your book available for sale online and in bookstores, where someone can purchase it, take it home, and read it. Publishing your book means it is now available for the world to order and read. It is distributed through a network that bookstores and libraries can purchase from and is available on Amazon and other book retailers.

Publisher Responsibilities

When you think about moving your story from a completed manuscript to a beautiful, published book, here are the six responsibilities to consider:

1. **Your Book Cover**

   - People judge a book by its cover. You want a book cover that you like and are proud of, but even more importantly, you want a book cover that encourages your reader to lean in and purchase the book. There's an art and a science to good book cover design.

2. **A Compelling Title and Subtitle**

   - There's a strategy to naming your book, based on buyer psychology and search engine optimization, so people can find your book. You want a title that people can remember and recommend, while also being clear so people know the promise of your book.

3. **The Editing Process**

   - I don't recommend that you edit your own work. Instead, it's important to have someone else review your manuscript, make structural suggestions(this is called developmental editing), and fix any small issues such as grammar, spelling, word use, and sentence flow (this is what we call copy editing).

4. **Format and Layout**

   - The next important step is to take your manuscript from a Google document and lay it out in a print-ready file so that it looks like the beautiful interior of a professionally published book. The format and layout of the book dramatically affect the reader's experience. Small decisions such as font, font size, line spacing, where the page number goes, and how call-out quotes appear can drastically improve or diminish the reader's experience.

5. **Print Quality**
   - The quality of the paper, the size of the book, and even the scent of the book really matter. You could have an incredibly well-written book but a poorly put-together book. It's important to care about every little detail so that you can put together a printed book that you can be proud of. I highly recommend having both a paperback and a hardcover edition available, plus a digital version for Kindle and other eBook readers.

6. **Distribution**
   - Make sure your book is easy to purchase. This means having or building relationships with major book retailers. Don't limit your book only to one retailer, but make sure it is available to local bookstores and independent bookstores. You want to work with a publisher who distributes your book the way other books are distributed, essentially allowing your book to be in a catalog where a librarian or a bookstore owner can order the book. You also want to make sure that your book is available on Amazon Prime, as at least 80% of all books are purchased from Amazon, usually with a Prime subscription. As an author, you don't want to have to worry about printing and shipping. This is the kind of thing that your publisher should worry about and take care of.

The Three Paths to Publication

Now let's talk about how to actually get your book published. Who is going to take care of the editing and formatting, the printing and the distribution, the book title and the cover design, and so much more? You have three options when it comes to publishing your book.

1. Traditional Publishing

With traditional publishing, a large, established publisher offers you a book publishing contract after receiving a compelling book proposal from you or your agent. Publishers often receive thousands of unsolicited proposals and are very selective about whom they decide to publish. In traditional publishing, the publisher takes on all the risk by financing the publication of your book, hoping to make a profit. As a result, the royalty percentage they offer you tends to highly favor the publisher. Essentially, they're putting up all the money to pay for the team and to publish your book, hoping to make back their money and more.

Most authors who get picked by a publisher have an agent, similar to a realtor, who represents and presents your book proposal to publishers. Agents work on commission, typically around 15% of any money you make from the book. They help you create a compelling book proposal and shop it around to their contacts in the publishing industry.

The process generally involves an acquisitions editor reviewing your proposal. If they decide to work with you, they will offer a publishing contract, leading to a negotiation between the publishing house and your agent. The timeline from securing an agent to landing a book deal can be about a year, followed by another year or more to write and launch the book. While this path offers credibility and extensive distribution, it can be highly competitive and lengthy. Moreover, traditional publishers look for authors with substantial followings, often expecting the ability to sell around 10,000 copies.

With traditional publishing:

- **They Pay, They Decide:** The publisher chooses who they'll publish, leading to a very high rejection rate because they're looking for well-known authors with a large and established audience, a significant social media following, and a substantial email list.

- **Royalties:** Often, traditional publishers offer a royalty rate of around 15% to 20% of the net profits. For example, if your book's net profit is $10, the publisher might make about $8.50 and you make $1.50 per book.

- **Control:** They take care of everything, including choosing your book title and cover. Many authors we've worked with at hope*writers have complained that the traditional publisher overrules them, picks a book cover they don't like, and changes their book title.

- **Benefits:** If your book sells a lot of copies or hits at the right moment, getting a traditional publishing deal can be amazing. Sometimes there's a large financial advance on royalties, and they can get you booked on large media shows to promote your book.

2. Self-Publishing

The second option is self-publishing, where you pick everything yourself. You control every aspect of your book's creation and distribution, akin to being the general contractor of your own house. You choose the cover designer, editor, and formatter, and you also manage the upload to platforms like Amazon and Barnes & Noble. Self-publishing can be incredibly rewarding if you have the skills or budget to handle these tasks.

One of the major benefits of this path is that you keep 100% of the profits, unlike traditional publishing, where you receive about 10-15% of the net profits. Self-publishing also allows for a faster timeline, potentially taking as little as three months. However, the challenge lies in maintaining quality. Many self-published books skimp on aspects like cover design and editing, leading to a less professional appearance. Ensuring your book doesn't look cheap requires investment in quality services instead of trying to do it all yourself.

Self-publishing has been around for as long as the printing press, but with the rise of digital printing technology, print-on-demand, and the ubiquity of Amazon, it has seen a resurgence. Anyone can simply take a Word document and, in about 30 minutes, upload that file to a print-on-demand site, click a few buttons, and have a book ready for sale.

Some factors to consider with self-publishing :

- **Control:** You're in charge of the entire process, including picking the book title, cover, editing, and marketing of the book. This process can feel very overwhelming if you want to do it right.

- **Quality vs. Speed:** If you're in a hurry, self-publishing is a great option. But if you want a professional-looking book, it can be quite complicated. Many self-published authors we've spoken with felt overwhelmed by the number of decisions and the skills needed to publish their book.

- **Financial Rewards:** You make all the decisions and keep all the money. If your book's net profit is $10, you get to keep all $10 without sharing it with a publisher.

3. Hope Publishing

The third option for publishing your book is a blend of traditional and self-publishing. We call this "hope publishing", though others have used the word "hybrid" to describe the mix of traditional and self-publishing.

At hope*books, we operate as a hybrid publisher, sharing the investment with you to provide a comprehensive and supportive publishing experience. Our goal is to help you discover, share, publish, and market your message through a step-by-step book management system that includes coaching, community, and a detailed video curriculum. Unlike traditional publishers, we do charge a fee for our services, but you get support each step of the way to help you write, publish, and launch a book that you are proud of!

What you get with hope*books:

- **Full-Service Publishing**: From book cover design to editorial work, layout, and listing on major platforms like Amazon and Barnes & Noble, we provide all the services of a traditional publisher.

- **Marketing Expertise:** We include marketing support to ensure your book reaches the right audience effectively, leveraging the expertise of our marketing team.

- **Book Landing Pages:** Our team creates a dedicated web page for your book, making it easy for people to learn about and purchase your book.

- **Ongoing Support:** We offer weekly group coaching with tips and strategies to maintain your book's momentum post-launch, supporting you through re-launches and continued promotion.

- **Creative Control:** You get to choose with hope*-books. It's your book and you maintain your copyright and creative control at all times. We want to make sure that your message remains true to your vision!

hope*books is here to guide you every step of the way, making your publishing journey smooth and rewarding. To learn more, visit hopebooks.com.

What Authors Are Saying About Working with hope*books

"As soon as I heard about hope*books, it immediately felt like the perfect fit for my needs. And it has been! hope*books is the full package, from development to cover design to marketing. It has pushed me just enough to keep me moving forward. I love the cohort and team support."

— Dawn W.

"My experience with hope*books has been truly rewarding. Being part of a like-minded community, I've found inspiration and valuable insights throughout the writing and publishing process. With hope*books, I've found the perfect platform to transform my vision into a reality while connecting with a supportive network of authors and professionals."

— Mark M.

"Previously overwhelmed and unable to pursue my passion for writing, hope*books provided guided steps, invaluable mentorship, and a supportive community. The experience has been transformative, freeing up my time to focus on writing while feeling supported and cared for. Thanks to hope*books, I now pursue my writing dreams with confidence and purpose."

— Lisa D.

Now it's your turn. Visit hopebooks.com to sign up today.

CONCLUSION

Your Legacy of Hope

I want you to picture yourself at 85 years old. Your family has moved you into an assisted living facility. Many of your friends, and maybe even your spouse, have already passed. You have time to think back on your life: the experiences you had, the friendships you made, the life you lived, and the memories you created.

As your great-grandchildren come to visit you, they ask to hear your story. They want to know what it was like to live in the early 21st century, before most of the modern technology they're used to today. They want to know about the challenges you faced in your life and how you overcame them. They want to know their history.

So you try your best to remember and share a story or two. The visit is short but incredibly meaningful.

Then, one of them says to you, "Grandma, I love that story because I read it in your book."

And then you remember. That's right. You shared your story in a book. As you begin to think and reflect, you realize the impact of sharing your hope*story. You remember all of the people whose lives were changed because you did the hard work of writing and publishing your book all those years ago.

An Invitation to You

Today you have a choice.

You can keep saying, "Someday I'll write and publish my book." Or . . . you can make that day today.

We would love to help you at hope*books.

It's because of you and your story that we started hope*books. Too often, great stories get overlooked by traditional publishers. And many first-time authors are simply overwhelmed by the self-publishing decisions. Hope*books takes the pain out of publishing, with a proven process to help you discover, share, and publish your message of hope.

Would you consider linking arms with us to help you finally publish your hope story? We would be honored to work with you.

Before we wrap up, I want you to imagine the legacy you could leave by writing and publishing your hope story. Picture all of the lives that could be touched. Envision the hope-filled words you could share for generations to come by finally writing and publishing your hope story.

Your legacy begins today.

Now is the time to decide.

Will you write and publish your book? Your future self, and countless others, will thank you.

Visit hopebooks.com to get started today.

Made in the USA
Columbia, SC
07 September 2024

41938383R00079